MAKING SHAPED BOOKS

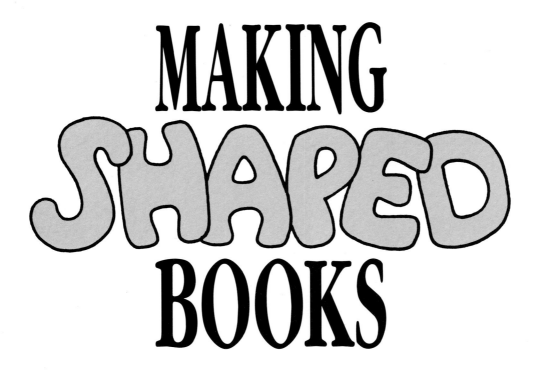

Gillian Chapman
Pam Robson

SIMON & SCHUSTER
YOUNG BOOKS

To the teachers and children of Kent
who participated with such enthusiasm
in our Making Books Workshops

Workshop photographs by Pam Robson

This book was prepared for
Simon & Schuster Young Books by
Globe Enterprises of Nantwich, Cheshire

Visualisation and book design: Gillian Chapman
Photography: Rupert Horrox

First published in Great Britain in 1993
by Simon & Schuster Young Books
Campus 400, Maylands Avenue
Hemel Hempstead, Herts HP2 7EZ

A catalogue record for this book is available
from the British Library
ISBN 0 7500 1391 5

Printed and bound in Hong Kong
by Wing King Tong Ltd

CONTENTS

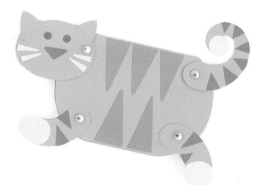

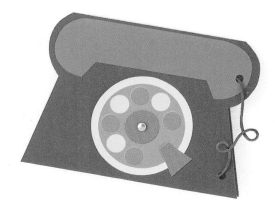

INTRODUCTION

The first shaped book was made over 500 years ago—it was a book of love songs in the shape of a heart. Its shape reflected exactly what was contained inside its pages. At about the same time in Mexico, decoratively painted zig-zag books were being made to record stories of legends and conquests.

Making shaped books is not a new idea, but it can be an original way to present information. You can have a lot of fun making the book and it certainly will be fun to read.

Before you Begin
Before you begin to make a shaped book, think about the type of book it is going to be. Will it hold fact or fiction—will it be about real or imaginary things? How many pages will it have? What shape will best suit your ideas? And most of all—who is going to read your book?

Using the Templates
You may wish to make one of the shaped books featured in this book. Most of the ideas have corresponding templates on pages 28-31. How to enlarge and use these template shapes is explained in detail on page 10. By using a template, every shaped book you make will be successful.

Mounting Words and Pictures.

Because this kind of book has pages of an unusual shape you will need to think about the best way to present your story. If you have chosen coloured pages you may decide to put your pictures and writing on to white paper first. Make sure it has been cut to a size that will fit nicely on to the coloured pages. You may choose to mount only the pictures, and write the words straight onto the coloured pages.

Whatever you decide, the secret is to plan carefully first and try to make your book as neat and attractive as you possibly can.

Paper Sizes

Paper is usually cut into a range of internationally recognised sizes known as the 'A' series. The largest size, A0, has an area of one square metre and measures 841 x 1189 mm. The other sizes in the series (A1, A2, A3, etc.) are each obtained by folding in half the previous size, as explained in this diagram.

A6 105 x 148 mm	**A5** 148 x 210 mm	**A3** 297 x 420 mm
A4 210 x 297 mm		
		A1 594 x 841 mm
A2 420 x 594 mm		

A0 841x 1189 mm

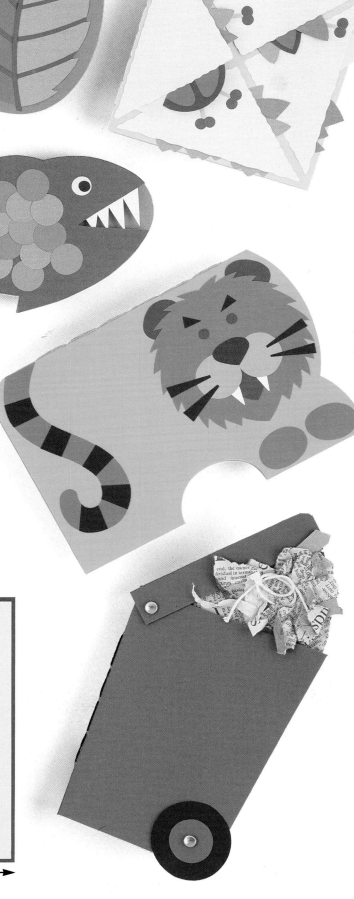

HOW TO MAKE A BOOK

Choosing the Materials

The type of paper you use to make your book is very important—not just the colour but the thickness and texture. The thicker the paper, the more difficult it is to fold and cut neatly. If you are making a shaped book using a template, you must cut through several sheets of folded paper. Feel the thickness of the paper first. Then pick colours that suit the theme of your book—you may decide on a different colour for each page. Choose a strong thread to sew the pages together.

Sewing Pages

Position the pages corner to corner and fold them exactly in half. Make a neat crease along the centre fold and open the pages again. Use paper-clips to hold the pages together at the corners. Place the centre fold in a horizontal position, as shown in the diagrams.

Measure the length of the centre fold and mark the middle with a dot. Measure sewing points, either side of the middle dot, about 2-3 cm apart, and mark these also. You must measure accurately. The number of points and the distance they are apart depends on the length of the centre fold, but there must be an *odd* number.

Sewing pages ▼

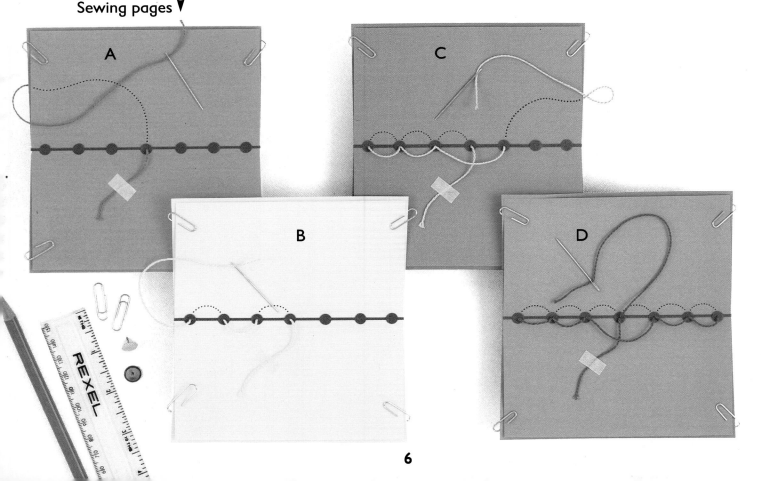

6

With a drawing pin prick through the dots you have marked to make the sewing holes. Thread a large, blunt-tipped needle with strong thread and start to sew at the middle hole. If your book has no cover start sewing from the inside, but if you intend to put a strong cover on the book start from the outside.

Use single thread and do not tie a knot. Pull it through the middle hole leaving an 8 cm tail. Hold it in place with a small piece of masking tape [A]. Start sewing in and out of the holes in one direction [B]. Continue to the end, then turn back, filling the gaps. When you reach the middle hole jump over it [C], then continue sewing to the other end.

Turn the book around and sew in the gaps, towards the centre. Pull the needle through the centre hole [D]. Remove the masking tape and tie a knot. Do not cut the ends too short.

This method of sewing can be used for a book with side sewing as shown below. If you choose very thick thread like string, wool or laces, you can make larger holes with a hole punch. Instead of cutting your threads, you could make them into tassels or a book mark.

There are many ways to bind pages together, like stapling or using binding rings—it is worth experimenting. However, sewing gives a strong, long-lasting result with a professional finish that is just like a real book.

Different thread and paper combinations

SIMPLE SHAPES

Designing a Shaped Book

If you are making a shaped book you will need to plan out your design first on paper. Think about the shape and size of the book and the format. A landscape format has the sewing along the shorter side of the book. A book with a portrait format is sewn together along the longer side. They make very different books.

Once you have planned the shape and format, decide where the line of stitches will begin and end along the centre fold. If you are using a template, it must be longer than the stitching line.

When cutting around the template you must not cut into the stitches, or your book will fall apart. This is why it is important to measure the sewing holes accurately, bearing in mind the *finished* shape of the book.

Making the Template

To make a template, measure and draw your shape on to card. Cut it out with a craft knife, using a cutting mat. Take time to cut the shape out carefully as the template will determine the shape of all the books you make from it.

landscape ▲
portrait ►

▼ Different format triangle-shaped books using the same template

Positioning the Template

When you have sewn the pages of your book together (see pages 6-7) remove the paper-clips from the corners. Close the book and replace the paper-clips. Make sure the fold line is clearly marked.

Position the template on top of the book and secure it with the paper-clips. Check that the stitches are inside the template shape. Draw around the template and unclip it from the book. Cut out the shape, making sure you are cutting through all the pages.

▶ Position the template and draw round it

Simple shapes

You can make an unusual book from a simple shape, as you can see from the examples on this page. Use any shape with straight sides. Shapes with curved sides can easily be adapted by flattening one side to allow for the sewing. The oval shape is very useful for mask and face-shaped books. You can even make a 2-D shape look 3-D, like the cube book.

FARM ANIMAL SHAPES

Size is very important in book design. It should suit the purpose and function of your book. How big will your book be? Is it intended to be a large information book to be read by many people, a tiny personal diary or a book of poetry?

Many of the designs featured in this book use the template shapes, which can be found on pages 28-31. Whether you design your own template shape or choose one from this book, you may need to enlarge it.

All the templates fit on to A7 paper. This means that they can easily be enlarged for a book made from A4 or A3 sized paper. If you have the use of a photocopier with an enlarger, it is very easy, otherwise use the following method.

Scaling up a Template

A4 is four times larger than A7. To enlarge an A7 template to A4, first trace the template on to centimetre squared paper. Then divide a piece of A4 tracing paper into 4 cm squares. There will be the same number of squares on the A7 paper as on the A4 paper, but they will be a different size.

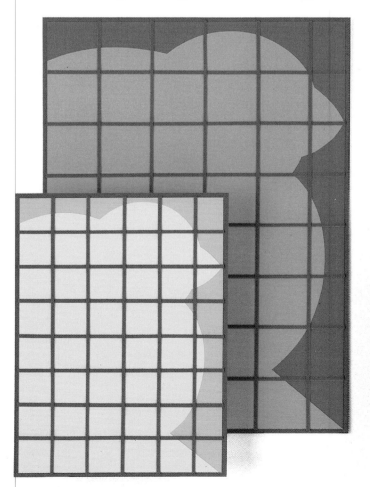

Scaling up the template ▲

▲ Different sized books from the same shape

Copying the Design

Transfer the A7 template design to the A4 tracing paper by copying it square by square. You now have a drawing of the enlarged design which can be traced directly onto card to make an A4 sized template.

Solid Shapes and Features

Look at these examples of Farm Animal Books and consider how each one was designed. Features, such as tails and ears, are within the template shape, rather than sticking out from it. The books have a solid shape with no bits that might bend or tear off.

Make small template shapes from tracings of heads and noses, if you find them difficult to draw neatly. Think about these details when you come to design your own shaped book as they make a big difference to the finished appearance.

▲ Small templates for
heads and features

11

WILD ANIMAL SHAPES

Most animal shapes can fit into both landscape and portrait formats. The finished shaped book works equally well with the sewing either along the length of the book, or along the side, as you can see from these examples.

Positioning the fold

Look carefully at the whole shape first, before deciding where to position the fold of the book. Sometimes the book's design and character is spoilt by straightening the curved side of an animal's shape. With the fish shape, the fold only works along the tail, to have it along the top of the fish would spoil the shape. With the bird book, the fold works successfully only along the back of the bird.

◄ Lion and tiger books same template different formats

◄ Different birds from the same template

Fish books—same shape, different size ►

Planning the Pages

It is extremely important to choose the format carefully. When you open a book, pages in a landscape format look completely different to those in a portrait format. This difference will affect the way in which you decide to mount the words and pictures, you intend to put inside.

Some papers or pages may be too large to mount in your shaped book. You may have extra information that you would prefer to store in a folder. Why not make a folder that matches your shaped book.

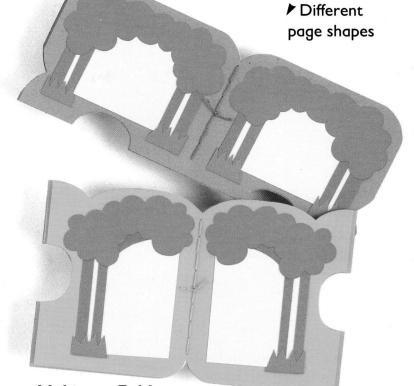

▶ Different page shapes

▼ Making a folder

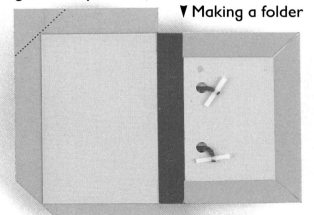

Shaped book and matching folder ◀

Making a Folder

Cut out two rectangles from scrap card—an empty cereal box is perfect. If you are making a folder to hold A4 papers, the rectangles of card should measure 25 x 34 cm.

Line up the two rectangles of card, leaving a 2 cm gap between them. Join them together with tape on the outside, folding about 4 cm of tape over the top and bottom. Cut a piece of tape the same length as the card and cover the gap between the rectangles, on the inside.

Make sure the plain side of the cereal box is on the inside of the folder. Cover the outside of the card with coloured paper, trimming the corners neatly. Punch holes in the card and thread treasury tags through to hold papers. Using the template you can decorate the folder to match your shaped book.

13

MOVING SHAPES

Many story books and information books tell of journeys and travel adventures. Making a shaped book about this is very simple and will make the book even more memorable.

Look at all the examples shown here. All types of transport—by air, sea or road—have special shapes. Again you will have to think about the format you choose. With many of these ideas only one format will work. Look at the train and rocket ideas.

Machines that move along the ground, or through water, probably suit a landscape format best. Machines that travel upwards, into the sky, generally suit a portrait format.

landscape ▲
portrait ►

Making Parts Move

The idea of moving along, or going on a journey, can be made more real by giving the book parts that move.

Cars and buses can have wheels that turn, submarines and boats can have propellers. Diggers have shovels that move up and down. Extra parts can be attached to the book using split pins. Take care when using these pins and remember to cover the sharp points with tape at the back.

All kinds of machine shapes, either real or imaginary, can be given moving parts. Let your imagination run riot and think up a story about a fantastic machine with moving cogs and levers, or a robot with arms and legs that go madly out of control.

▲ Use split pins to make moving wheels

BUILDING SHAPES

Planning the Book
More adventurous and complicated shaped books, with extra devices such as moving parts or pop-out flaps, need more planning to make sure the book is really successful.

If you are spending a long time on one book it makes sense to take special care. It may be worth making a 'dummy' book first. That is the complete book in rough form. Only then will you discover any problems and pitfalls and be able to correct them before making the final book.

Structure and Size
Buildings suggest some very interesting book designs because there are so many different shapes and sizes from which to choose—from huge impressive skyscrapers and cathedrals to small bungalows and caravans. Roofs and window shapes vary all over the world, depending on the climate and geography.

Try to relate the format of the book to the actual shape of the building, if you can. However, not every design works—some are too awkward to cut out and are best kept within a simpler shape, like the mosque book shown here. The arch shape in the mosque has been cut through the inside pages of the book.

Castle 'dummy' book ▼

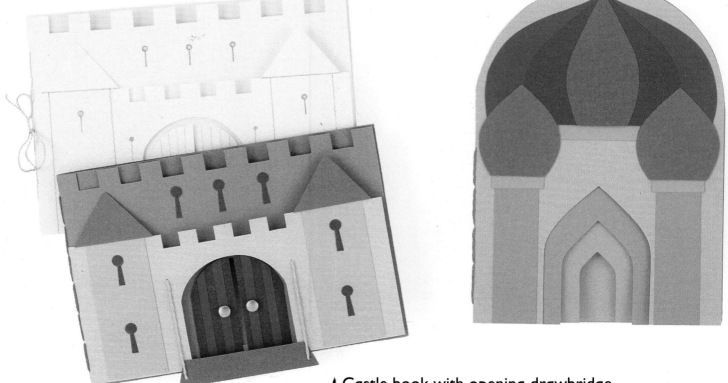

▲ Castle book with opening drawbridge and doors

16

Door and Window Flaps

Once the overall shape has been planned, then you can have fun with the details. Perhaps the building could have opening windows and doors. These features will need planning. Think carefully before you position an opening flap. Do not put it too close to the edge of the page as a thin strip will be left that could easily become torn.

Decoration and Detail

Decorating the building gives plenty of scope for experimenting with patterns and texture. You can attach roof tiles, curtains, shutters, drainpipes and chimney pots using all kinds of collage materials.

A thin strip, like the one to the right of the door, will tear easily ►

Thin strip ◄

GREEN SHAPES

If you are writing about conservation or environmental issues, you could make a 'green' book to contain your work. Not only can the shape of the book reflect the conservation theme, but the book itself can be made from recycled materials. Old cardboard boxes and food packaging can all be used.

Making a 'Green' Book
Make the book as explained on page 6, but try using newspaper, thin packaging or even plastic for the pages. Sew the book together with wool or string.

Conservation
Your green book could cover global problems, such as the destruction of the rainforests and the ozone layer, but local problems are equally important. Books shaped like cans or bins could be used for information about local recycling projects, such as bottle banks and litter surveys.

▼ 'Green' books made from recycled paper and string

Can books and bin books for recycling projects

Collage and Texture

The recycling theme can be emphasised by using 'junk' materials to create special effects, illustrating the conservation message while at the same time decorating the cover.

Use only discarded fabrics and papers, like sweet wrappers and torn magazine pictures, to make colourful collages. Plastic, foil and cloth also give interesting textures.

Newspaper
▶tree book

Rainforest book with magazine picture collage ▼

▼ Parrot book with sweet wrapper design

Turtle book with fabric shell◀

Patterns from Everyday Rubbish!

Multi-coloured patterns can make striking cover designs, especially if they are made from familiar advertisements and packaging. Arrange the materials in a random patchwork, use anything bright, and wait to see the reaction of your readers!

▲ Patterns with packaging

19

SYMMETRICAL SHAPES

When a symmetrical shape is folded in half, it is exactly the same on either side of the fold. Any shape like this can be used to make an open book. Simple shapes work best. 'Flying' shapes, where the wings become the pages of the book, work very well. Making a symmetrical shaped book is slightly different because the book is designed to remain open with a set of pages on each side.

Design and Decoration
Because the sewing threads are visible they can be an attractive feature of the design. Use colourful threads twisted or plaited together, making the sewing holes larger if necessary. Decorate the cover with coloured paper shapes and collage materials. The butterfly book has been sewn together from the top of the book, so the ends of the thread form its antennae.

Making a Symmetrical Book
Take your sheets of paper and fold them in half. Then clip them at the corners. Make a sharp crease along the centre fold. Open the pages and measure a row of dots along the centre fold, about 2-3 cm apart. Because this book is sewn together simply using a running stitch, it does not matter how many sewing holes there are.

Sewing down the Centre Fold
Prick through the dots using a drawing pin. Start at the bottom of the pages sewing in and out of the holes. When you reach the bottom again, tie a knot and cut off the ends.

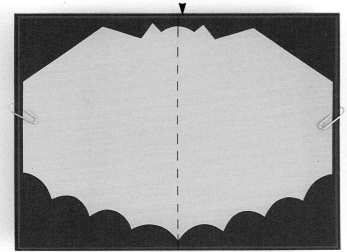

centre fold

Positioning the template ▲

Positioning the Template

Place the template on the open sewn pages, using the paper-clips to hold it in place. Make sure the clips are clear of the edge of the template to be cut, otherwise you won't be able to draw round it properly. Cut out the symmetrical shape, making sure you are cutting through all the pages together. Do not cut through the stitching line.

Shaped Pages Inside a Cover

You may want to make a strong cover for the shaped pages, especially if they are intricately cut and would be better protected by a cover. If you intend to have a cover you must add an extra rectangular page to the outside of the shaped pages before sewing them. Make the rectangular page slightly larger and sew all the pages together as explained before. Start sewing from the outside of the centre fold so the knotted thread will be hidden by the cover.

Making the Cover

Take two pieces of scrap card and, leaving a 2 cm gap between, join them together using hessian or tape. The cards need to be about 1 cm larger all round than the rectangular page. Cover the cards with coloured paper, as shown on page 13. Place the sewn pages on the cover and glue down the rectangular pages, as shown below.

rectangular page ◄

If you start sewing
the shaped page at the top, you can use
the threads as a bookmark ◄

ZIG-ZAG SHAPES

Zig-zag books are clever visual books, showing pictures that need only a few words for the best effect. They can be almost any shape, but because the zig-zag folds out to make a long shape, some ideas work better than others. Designs that stretch out are ideal, such as caterpillars, trains, herds of animals or parades.

▶ Straighten up both sides of the template

Adapting the Template

Many of the template shapes shown in this book can be used to make zig-zag books. Some will need to be adapted so they have two flat sides. This is important if the book is to fold correctly.

A3 sheet of paper

Measuring and Folding the Paper

Depending on the length of the zig-zag book and how many pages it will have, you may have to join several pieces of paper together. If an A3 size sheet of paper is folded and cut into quarters, it will make four pages for an A5 zig-zag book. If it is folded and cut into eight, it will make a small A6 book.

A5 size pages

Check the thickness of the paper first before too many pages are folded, because they will all have to be cut through together. Use a fairly thick paper so that the book will stand upright when it is stretched open.

A6 size pages

tape

Cutting out the Shape

Once the paper is folded the template can be positioned, using paper-clips to hold it in place while you are drawing around it. You must take care not to cut along the folded sides, or the book will fall apart.

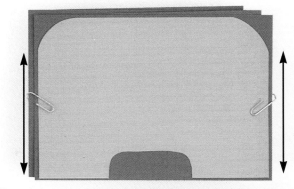

▲ Do not cut on the folds between the arrows

With all zig-zag designs the character of the book changes from a single image when the book is closed, to a whole row when the book is stretched open. A single tree grows into a forest and a lorry becomes a long convoy.

MINI-SHAPES

➤Mini-book template

Sometimes you only need a little book to write in. Maybe you are writing about something small that needs a little book all of its own. A mini-book can be a little picture book or a poetry book, or it might even be a secret diary. You could make one as a gift for someone special. A mini-book will easily slip into a envelope and makes a lovely surprise present!

The mini-books on these pages are only 14 cm long. They are all made using the template shown here. It is the actual size needed, so it can be traced directly from the page.

◄ 14 cm

◄ 5 sewing holes, 2 cm apart

How to Make Mini-Books

Use two or three sheets of A5 paper folded in half, so the final size of the mini-book will be A6.

Measure the sewing holes along the centre fold. You will only need five holes, positioned 2 cm apart. Prick through the holes and sew the pages together, as explained on pages 6-7.

Position the template carefully, holding it in place with two small paper-clips. Draw around it and cut out the shaped mini-book. Use small sharp scissors for cutting rather than a craft knife and take care. With little books any slight unevenness shows.

2 cm

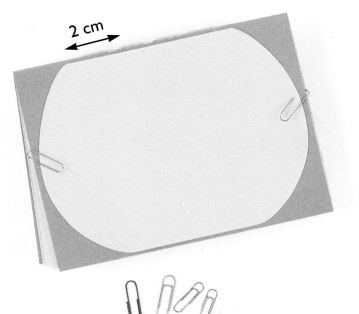

Now you can have fun designing the cover. Look at all the ideas shown below. Mini-beasts are an ideal subject for mini-books. There are many tiny creatures that might feature in a story—spiders, beetles, ladybirds, and snails—as well as flowers, leaves and shells.

Because mini-book pages are so small, you will need to think very carefully about the words and pictures you put inside. You could make a set of mini-books covering a similar theme and match it with a large book. For example, if you were writing about trees, make a large tree-shaped book and have acorn, leaf and mushroom mini-books to accompany it.

MY SHAPE

It is useful to have a way of keeping information about ourselves for future reference—memories are not very reliable! It can be fun to look back and read about past events. After all, books help us to learn and remember about the past.

Personal Books

If you are writing about yourself, you could keep all your information in a diary or personal record book. A diary is a book of words and it may be better to keep it as a rectangle, but you may choose to decorate the cover with shapes that are personal to you—maybe your portrait or silhouette?

You can also have fun designing and making books to store useful information, such as favourite recipes or friends' addresses and telephone numbers.

Shaped Scrapbooks

Everyone collects something.
The problem is always where to keep the collection. Shaped scrapbooks are an ideal way of storing treasured cuttings, postcards, tickets and pamphlets. It is important to make a collection look attractive, then it becomes interesting to others.

The pyramid shaped book started as rectangular pages, sewn along two diagonals, as shown here. It would make an ideal book in which to record a visit to a museum or an ancient monument.

A collection relating to a particular sport or hobby can be organised into a suitable shaped book. If you need a larger format to store extra sheets of paper, make a matching folder, as explained on page 13.

Trainer book and
matching folder ◄

TEMPLATE SHAPES 1

All the template shapes on these pages fit on to A7 paper, that is a piece of paper measuring 105 x 74 mm. To make these templates fit an A4 piece of paper they will need to be enlarged four times.

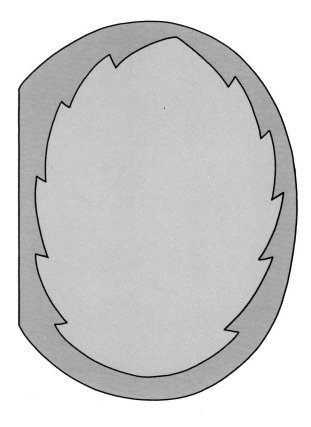

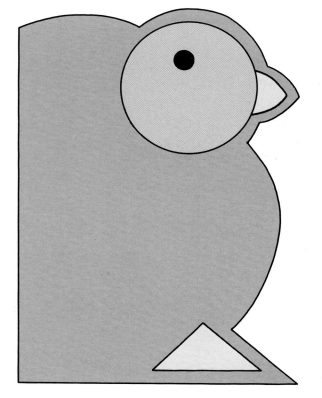

28

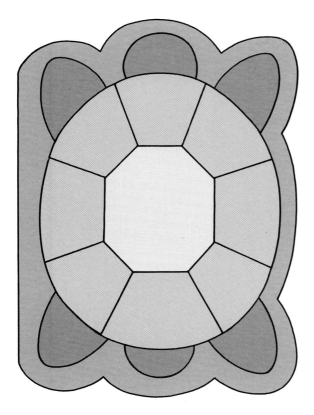

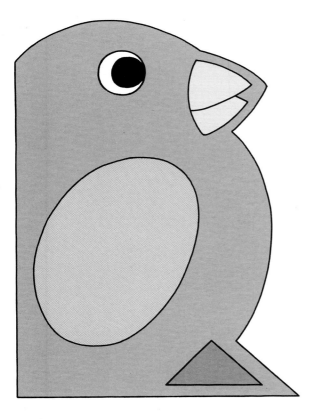

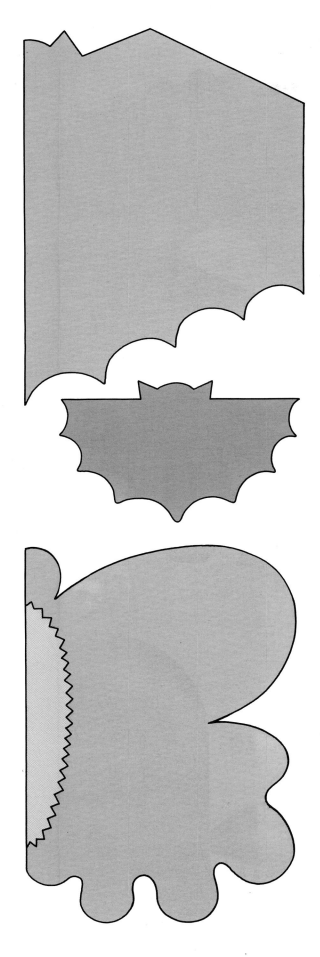
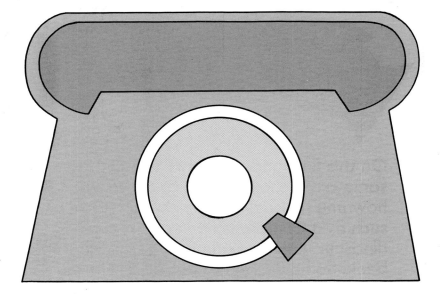

CRAZY SHAPES

On this final page we have included some crazy shapes—just to show how any unusual idea or character, such as a Chinese dragon or a dinosaur, can be made into a shaped book. Some designs will obviously need careful thought and planning, but we hope we have inspired you to have fun putting your ideas into practice!

Making a Library

We hope that you will make many shaped books for your own stories, poems and pictures. Think about making a library of your books. Arrange them altogether on a shelf in your room so that your friends and family can enjoy seeing and reading them.

Make a library of your books